A COLLECTION OF VERSE

J. B. Dundee

ARTHUR H. STOCKWELL LTD
Torrs Park, Ilfracombe, Devon, EX34 8BA
Established 1898
www.ahstockwell.co.uk

© *J. B. Dundee, 2019*
First published in Great Britain, 2019

The moral rights of the author have been asserted.

All rights reserved.
No part of this publication may be reproduced
or transmitted in any form or by any means,
electronic or mechanical, including photocopy,
recording, or any information storage and
retrieval system, without permission
in writing from the copyright holder.

British Library Cataloguing-in-Publication Data.
A catalogue record for this book is available
from the British Library.

DEDICATION

To my parents, George and Rosemary, and my wife, Gillian.

ISBN 978-0-7223-4918-2
Printed in Great Britain by
Arthur H. Stockwell Ltd
Torrs Park   Ilfracombe
Devon EX34 8BA

CONTENTS

Living for Dreams	5
Tunnel of Darkness	6
A Merry Christmas	7
Greed	8
Pot of Gold	9
Life's Secret	10
These Clowns	11
Grey Streets	12
Everyone's Friend	13
The Poet's Dream	14
Ode to Spring	15
This Park	16
Moorland Tavern	17
You People	18
Rainy Day	19
Man-o'-War	20
Memories	21
Jet-Set Days	22
Fair Lady	23
In the Still of the Night	24
Lucky the Man	25
Inspiration	26
You're the Key	27
Personal Thoughts	28
Material Wealth	29
Biding My Time	30
Morning	31
Angel from Above	32
Beautiful Nature	33
Sleepy Sunday	34
Dear Sue	35
Human Beings	36
Teenage Disaster	37
Peaceful Companion	38
This Empty Man	39
Resplendent Within Reputation	40

Twentieth Century Legend	41
Cat-and-Mouse Game	42
The Soldier's Lament	43
The Gambler	44
Styal Trial	45
Thoughtless Few	46
Drinking Man's Plight	47
Tomorrow	48
Train to Freedom	49
Soon	50
Inspiration from the Past	51
Divine Exemption	52
The Union Card	53
Winter-Morning Blues	54
The Cat and the Lion	55
The Death of a Poet	56
A Faith Betrayed	57
True Escape	58
The Foulest of Four-Letter Words	59
Unsuspecting Angels	60
Stunning Charm	61
Helpless Situation	62
Peer's Pest	63
Without You	64

LIVING FOR DREAMS

Mock not the daydreamer
sleeping on in his bed;
there's a life of contentment
quite real in his head.

'Tis a way of escaping
reality's fears,
to a world of his making,
without many tears.

Some say he is lazy,
there is no time to lose,
whilst they are busy rushing
or standing in queues.

For him life's not frantic;
ambitions, he's none.
He is quite happy dreaming
in the afternoon sun.

Some think it be pointless,
just living for dreams.
Life has got to be active;
at least that's how it seems.

But as they approach their last day,
with his dreams and their strife,
just look back and consider
who's had the 'happiest' life.

TUNNEL OF DARKNESS

Static time as the seconds go passing.
Little to do but contemplate nothing.
Boredom like paralysis creeps through body and mind.
In a world of two rooms, wandering blind.
A soulless zombie, wasting breath.
Filling the space from birth to death.

In a tunnel of darkness, lost and hoping.
The light at the end no nearer approaching.
An empty existence disturbed by life.
A solitary feeling that cuts like a knife.
Noise of activity all about, out of reach.
No one to blame, accuse and impeach.

A MERRY CHRISTMAS

The lights upon the Christmas tree flash colours through the room.
Decorations cover every wall.
Street light through the frost stretches out into the gloom
as from the heavens sparkling snowflakes fall.

It's a time of endless parties, pretty girls and mistletoe.
A festive spirit lives throughout the land.
Or sit around the fire with its warm and friendly glow,
dreaming with your loved one, hand in hand.

The church upon the hilltop resting noble in the snow,
with stars above it shining down so bright.
Children are in bed, hardly sleeping for they know
the man who brings their dreams will call tonight.

While they lie there dreaming in the middle of the night,
does the sound of sleigh bells echo in the sky?
If they look out of their window might they even catch a sight
of Santa and his reindeer flying by?

Looking forward to the presents and the programmes on the screen,
the films and Christmas specials on the set –
receiving cards from friends who are no longer seen,
though at this time of year you don't forget.

So to everyone around me, with a heart of glowing cheer,
I wish you all a merry Christmas Day.
As we celebrate, share a joke or shed a happy tear,
I hope with health and friends you'll always stay.

GREED

Greed sows the seed of destruction.
Greed paves the road to despair.
Just stop, look around, how we're living.
Learn how to help and to care.

Greed never ends – it surrounds us.
Greed haunts the young and the old.
As I see how this illness affects us,
the shame deep inside leaves me cold.

Greed has insatiable hunger.
Greed makes the best of us bad.
When I witness what lengths people go to,
for the whole human race I feel sad.

POT OF GOLD

Let us share once more the good times.
Let us relive all the fun,
when we couldn't talk for laughing
as we lounged beneath the sun.
I can still recall so clearly
all the manic things we've done,
through holidays and schooldays
and the booze when twenty-one.
All the people that I've known so well
and friends I've yet to meet –
I thank the Lord you're living
for you make my life complete.
Though the years pass by
and we go our separate ways,
let us never lose our pot of gold –
the memories of our days.
From Cornwall to Romania,
under dark or sunny sky,
when I'm looking at the photographs
I'd laugh until I cry.
However fate may treat me as
life goes from day to day,
however far I've travelled,
in my thoughts you'll always stay.
So here's to you, old friends and new,
for meeting you I'm glad.
You've given me without a doubt
the best times I've ever had.

LIFE'S SECRET

A lifetime is but a teardrop in the ocean.
You close your eyes and, to your surprise,
when they open your time is nearly over.
The wax of your candle burns slowly away.
You always know some day you will go,
but part of life's secret is when?

THESE CLOWNS

What's it all about with these clowns called politicians?
The only thing they seem to do is fulfil their own ambitions.
I know nothing of economy, but I know what's right and wrong.
I see the poor getting weak and the rich getting strong.
With lifeless eyes and lying tongue they feed us all the crap.
If we sit in dust and fight for a crust, we'll soon be back on the map.
But they're all right, still feast every night; they sit at the top of the pile.
They say it's tough, but they've got enough, with sincere and sickly smile.
It's a part of life I don't think I will ever understand.
I only know the burdens of life are resting in their hands.
So the next time you see a dog in the street, don't kick it out the way.
For all you know, that dog might grow to run the government one day.
The world of politics makes me ill; the whole thing's such a farce.
They run your life and twist the knife as they sit there on their arse.
They know nothing of the real world, the families trying to live.
They know only how to take and have forgotten how to give.

GREY STREETS

Grey streets with grey faces,
these poor hopeless places –
an existence unknown by the rich,
in a damp, dirty slum
where they would kill for a crumb,
like a land cruelly cursed by a witch.

The rats prosper only.
The children play, lonely.
For them life looks grim and forlorn.
They will not know life's pleasures,
have no share of its treasures,
dressed in rags from the moment they're born.

EVERYONE'S FRIEND

You walk around like a king.
You think you know everything.
You think you're so clever.
Be friends with you? Never!
Think you can tell a good joke?
I wish you'd bloody well choke.
You're a disease, feller.
You are a worst-seller.
If I had to spend a day with you I'd break your neck.
May be even sent away for it, but what the heck!
It would be worth it.
You've got a face like a tomb.
I'll have to leave this room –
you make me feel sick.
Man, you're so thick.
You'd have to take off and run
if I could get me a gun;
if you were still about,
I'd blow your brains out.
If the midwife could have known that you'd be such a clown,
she should have stuck you in the sink and let you damn well drown.
But now it's too late.
Think you're the life and soul?
Think you're the mint with the hole?
You think you're so cool.
You look a right fool –
try to be everyone's friend
and drive them all round the bend.
Not of the human race,
you're a headcase.
One day you're going to realise and maybe take the hint,
as far as wealth of friendship goes you're well and truly skint.
You're a pauper.
Though things in life at times go wrong
and leave me sitting here all blue,
I can always think, to cheer me up,
at least I'll never be like you.

THE POET'S DREAM

My eyes could never hope to see
another woman quite like she.
Her youthful smile and locks of blonde
do with my heart and soul abscond.

Her voice could calm hell's raging fires.
A breath of freshness she inspires.
The poet's dream, she walks this land,
an idyllic angel, truly grand.

She is all a mortal man could ask –
to seek yet more, a hopeless task –
a rainbow in my life's grey sky
to humbly grace and pacify.

ODE TO SPRING

Do my eyes deceive? Is that the sun I see?
The ground is dry – can this really be?
Clouds are white – I know not what to do.
The air is warm; my God, the sky is blue!

THIS PARK

I have roamed this park for many a year,
through sunshine, rain and snow,
from the highest hill, overlooking the land,
to the sheltered woods below.

In my youth, with my friends, we would talk and play
in imagined lands and times
while the clock at the stables echoed aloft,
resounding, haunting chimes.

I've seen the sun raise its head in the morning mist –
amber rays through the tops of the trees –
then at dusk bowing down in the deep-red west
in the chill of the sharp evening breeze.

Heaton Mansion rich and grand,
a monument to days gone by,
once a home, now museum of long-ago styles.
This park has many treasures for the eye.

Through summer green and autumn gold,
I have grown up in this park.
I feel I know it inch by inch –
each flower, each leaf, each bark.

Down meandering paths with my parents I stroll,
beneath the changing sky.
The only sounds are the rustling of trees in the wind
and the chirping of birds as they fly.

From tramway track to duck-lived lake,
I have walked on many a day.
It is all these thoughts, plus countless more,
in my mind will always stay.

MOORLAND TAVERN

Music plays and glasses clatter.
The murmuring sounds of idle chatter.
Soothing wall lamps red, so mellow,
mingle with the flames of the log fire yellow.
Beyond the window the wind is wailing.
The lashing of rain as the light is failing.
Along the roof of the tavern stretch firm wooden beams.
On the walls hang old pictures of long-ago scenes.
The old clock stands chimeless
in an atmosphere timeless
and cities seem part of some strange hazy dream.

YOU PEOPLE

In the morning I awake
to a world of calamity.
Just how much more can we take
before we lose our sanity?

Everyone is running round,
but time is running faster.
Soon will we all be in the ground.
Immortality has no master.

The noises in the street outside
grow louder by the minute.
I wish I could find a place to hide
and wall myself up in it.

Tempus fugit, so they say,
and death comes to us all.
Innocent children sit and play –
one day they too will fall.

Our world grows smaller year by year;
the sides are closing in.
When will we rid the lands of fear
and repent our race's sin?

The land and nature you destroy,
you people progress-mad.
But our earth forgives use as a toy;
for that we should be glad.

RAINY DAY

The trees are bare, with fingers reaching;
their bodies sway in the dull grey light.
Hedgerows dance with the swirling wind,
while sparrows pass by in erratic flight.

Their singing carries through the air
as the rain falls down to its grassy bed.
Dark clouds above, so low and heavy.
To drier pastures have the rabbits fled.

MAN-O'-WAR

To kill and be killed's not my idea of fun,
or staring down the barrel of some foreign soldier's gun.
Bullets they are whistling, but I don't like tune.
I would look so out of place in a fighting-fit platoon.

I confess here and now, a hero I am not.
My feet would kick up dust at the first sound of a shot.
Forget old battle movies – there's no glamour found in war.
You could kill your fellow man, never knowing what it's for.

I would so hate to be wounded – just think of all the pain.
Don't look my way for courage; if you do you are insane.
To call me a coward would only suit me fine.
It goes well with the yellow streak running down my spine.

If ever I'm conscripted, the shock would spin my head.
You would have to use a crowbar to dislodge me from my bed.
I would never earn a medal – I have no wish to be brave.
To heroics I'm a stranger, but to cowardice a slave.

MEMORIES

You tried your best, did all you could,
but soon she had departed.
Although you knew the end was near
you still felt broken-hearted.

One day you will forget her
and the tears will flow no more.
The skies will seem much brighter,
the memories not as sore.

JET-SET DAYS

The papers told the story
in the old familiar way –
of those with wealth and glory,
who threw it all away.

The world is theirs to conquer,
lying right before their feet,
while the poor look on in wonder,
with their lives so incomplete.

People waiting on them to serve,
upon a silver tray,
a bigger slice of cake than they deserve,
while abusing their position by the day.

For most it is a dream –
the world is there for them to use.
In society they're the cream,
but good fortune and their minds they abuse.

It seems to be the fashion,
when they've made it to the top.
A pop star or a princess –
once begun they rarely stop.

To fill their head with drugs the thing to do,
slowly to destroy a life so grand.
Then very soon their jet-set days are through,
their reasoning hard to understand.

FAIR LADY

By chance to glance at yonder beauty
is to gaze unto an angelic dream.
A maiden blessed with heaven's treasures –
fair lady crowned with love's esteem.

A flower rare from nature's garden,
sweet princess of the sun's embrace.
An apparition to behold –
a form of pure enchanting grace.

IN THE STILL OF THE NIGHT

My journey home in the still of night
is such an eerie, lonely task.
Thoughts of mugging and the supernatural
wander through my cautious mind.
The air is sharp on this damp spring eve;
a breeze blows soft and fresh.
As I walk down quiet lifeless streets,
around each corner what will I find?

My eyes see the world in black and white,
with splash of yellow shade.
A passing car is a comforting sign
that I am not the only one.
The street is bare – no children play;
the birds have disappeared.
How different this is to when the land is greeted
by the rays of the morning sun!

LUCKY THE MAN

Lucky the man with friendship dear;
he'll know not solitude when they're near.
They will bear his sorrow, share his joy
and make him wise to any ploy.

Lucky the man with friendship dear;
they'll mop his brow, dispel his fear.
Through times uncertain, times confused,
he'll never have his faith abused.

Lucky the man with friendship dear;
he will rarely shed a lonely tear.
Down saddened paths they'll take his arm
and keep him safe, away from harm.

Lucky the man with friendship dear;
they will always lend a thoughtful ear,
to rally round in times of need;
for help he'll never have to plead.

Lucky the man with friendship dear;
In his bleakest moment, their light shines clear.
If in life's bed of thorns he fell,
they'd tend his wounds and see him well.

Lucky the man with friendship dear;
his hours of gloom will disappear.
Though years go by and far they wander,
they'll have from their days no memories fonder.

Lucky the man with friendship dear;
the precious gift of friends sincere.
This land would be a soulless place
without a loyal smiling face.

INSPIRATION

Inspiration is a bastard –
it leads a merry dance,
to strike when unexpected
or perhaps to show by chance.

A passing urge that tempts you
to express your thoughts in verse.
Obscure or controversial,
in its world you soon immerse.

With a mind forever restless,
in the search for hidden views,
you spend your lonely hours
a helpless slave within the muse.

Only when the curse is lifted
can your modest way resume.
And from the toil of your conception
satisfaction's sweet perfume.

YOU'RE THE KEY

You make me smile when I'm feeling low.
How you mean the world to me!
What I would do without you I do not know.
To unlock my heart you're the key.

If ever I could make a wish,
just one would be divine.
The wish I would make with all my heart
is that forever you'd be mine.

I could never live without you.
With you my love is found.
I can't bear that lonely feeling
when you are not around.

I hope from my sight you will never stray.
You are all that I desire –
for you to be with me day by day.
Of you I'll never tire.

I would sell my soul to make you mine.
Without you I'd be lost.
I long for you till the end of time,
no matter what the cost.

I wouldn't care how you appear to me –
I will take you as you are.
So won't you listen to my plea
and never drift too far!

PERSONAL THOUGHTS

I seem to spend most of my life freezing
in the cold,
with icy shivers running down my spine.
There's so many things I'd like to do
before I get too old.
To be a millionaire would suit me fine.

I sometimes try to plan my life –
things rarely turn out right.
The course of life is one of constant grief –
an endless war with good and bad.
Which one will win the fight?
The unworthy get the best is my belief.

Good friendship is the fruit of life.
Denied it, we'd be lost –
this world would seem a jungle void of hope.
My kinsfolk mean the most to me –
they melt away the frost.
Without them I don't think that I could cope.

It doesn't matter what I do,
my worries hold me back.
I find a lack of nerve my greatest curse,
but with pride and self-devotion,
though things look grim and black,
I prefer that on my own my wounds I'll nurse.

MATERIAL WEALTH

Judge not the man by his material wealth.
It's not his status in life that's important,
but the man himself.
He may be well spoken and smartly dressed,
but with a dull personality that leaves you depressed.

Don't look down on the beggar,
with his hat clutched in hand.
There is more to good people, all too few understand.
Despite his shabby appearance, there may beat a heart of gold.
A soul of caring compassion.
A true human being to behold.

BIDING MY TIME

After fancy words and all the shovelling above,
here in the ground they rest my weary bones.
What a noisy affair, enough to wake the dead,
with the pounding on my lid of falling stones!
I should have gone for cremation – just think of the heat.
Then stuck on a shelf, watching telly.
Instead I'm biding my time, turning to slime,
with black soil everywhere, damp and smelly.
I hear the worms and creatures kick up hell outside.
I hope this wood doesn't rot before me.
It's so claustrophobic stuck inside this padded box,
waiting here for when my spirit is set free.
Once the lads in purgatory have checked my file
to see which way I'm due to go,
only then will they let me leave this mouldy corpse
that people on the surface used to know.
I pray my neighbours aren't the noisy type.
I hate folk disturbing me while I rest.
After all, it's not so easy for me to move elsewhere
and when I get called upstairs I want to look my best.

MORNING

The morning mourns departed night.
The rising sun spreads its warm embrace.
Waking birds serenade the sky.
Dewdrops sparkle, soon to leave no trace.

Animals raise their weary heads;
neath a newborn virgin sky they yawn.
And so another day matures,
from the sleepy cradle of the eastern dawn.

ANGEL FROM ABOVE

I was no more than a boy when you walked into my life;
barely could I believe my staring eyes.
I knew only in my dreams I could hold you as my wife.
In disbelief you took me by surprise.

In a purple shroud you appeared, my angel from above,
thoughts for me not confided in your face.
From that moment I was lost. You will always be my love.
Till time's end not a soul could take your place.

Whenever I might get the chance I'd be there by your side.
With you I was as shackled as a slave.
A walk with you in public filled my heart with glowing pride,
to carry fond memories to the grave.

Only when you were about me, my daytime seemed worthwhile.
Without you sunny skies would fade away.
It made me feel so happy just to see your pretty smile.
With you I wish that I could always stay.

After all this time has passed us by, feelings still are true,
even though, my dearest, you are now wed.
And like a child away from home I long once more for you.
Your voice and laughter echo in my head.

To explain your company in a sound, coherent way
and express my heart's difficult to do.
I know this honour I will feel until my final day,
to have met one as beautiful as you.

BEAUTIFUL NATURE

People say nature's a beautiful thing –
the flowers in summer and joys of spring.
But tell that to the creatures being eaten alive.
The day-to-day terror as they try to survive.

God's little creatures can't enjoy the sights.
They're too busy running from predators' bites.
The cruelty and carnage on land, sea and air
make man's sins look tame when you stop and compare.

It's part of life's cycle to catch and to eat.
For blood-curdling horror, wildlife you can't beat.
The strongest live longest; the weak ones will die.
That's 'beautiful' nature – don't ask me why.

SLEEPY SUNDAY

Why is it when I feel so good my life just lets me down?
When I think I have it all worked out, in a pool of doubt I drown.
So I lie on sleepy Sunday in the comfort of my bed,
with the world outside so hectic as I crawl inside my head.

I long to be the drummer in a rock-and-roll band,
or maybe an explorer in a far and dangerous land.
Racing round a circuit, hear the turbo engine scream.
Perhaps a famous player for a top-class football team.
One day I'll be appearing on a show about my life,
sitting, reminiscing, with my family, friends and wife.
A DJ on the radio being heard throughout the land.
Acting on the big screen, with Kalashnikov in hand.
Boxing for the title, the opponent starts to tire.
A fireman on a ladder, fighting off a raging fire.
Some day you're going to see me a on a TV chat show
and maybe with an OBE, you never know.
Another prized photographer, taking photos praised by all.
A stuntman in a Western, thrown from a window in a brawl.
A face well known to millions, BBC and ITV,
or even on a freighter battling through a stormy sea.

The fog it clears, the radio's on, it's time to start my day.
The rain falls down; a rainbow's in the sky.
When I recall the things I've done, wouldn't change them any way.
The lives I lead beyond my resting eyes.

So I lie on sleepy Sunday in the comfort of my bed,
with the world outside so hectic as I crawl inside my head.

DEAR SUE

To the girl who brightens up my weary life,
let me wish you every joy beneath the sun.
It is a happy occasion, to be shared with friends,
on this special day that sees you twenty-one.

My warmest greetings and affection this fine August day,
from the bottom of my heart I send to you.
May your coming years be happy; may you never feel alone.
All these things and more I wish for you, dear Sue.

HUMAN BEINGS

The cards in life's game are dealt without favour.
You just use what you're given as best as you can.
For some the taste of success is an unknown flavour.
But, wherever fate leads you, be a peace-loving man.

People fight for ideals, all around.
Those with guilt but no shame have their say.
There is death and despair to be found.
Can't they see towards oblivion we stray?

For religion and politics there are those who will kill.
For the sake of their colour, men are chosen to die.
It's such a useless waste, so pointless, yet still
this madness continues. Why?

We are all human beings with one chance at life.
There's so much good for mankind we could do.
The long road to the future has two ways: peace or strife.
On which one we embark's up to you.

TEENAGE DISASTER

It's no fun being called 'Spotty',
all covered in zits.
They get on your back,
then get on your tits.
Life's just one big blackhead
when your glands go berserk.
If a boil bursts in public
you feel such a jerk.
Your skin's marked forever,
a landscape of scars,
with a face full of craters,
like a monster from Mars.
With your acne pulsating,
all throbbing and hot,
when you're aching from squeezing
that pus-pumping spot.
It's a teenage disaster –
you can't bear to be seen.
You've a face like a pizza,
trying to keep your mind clean.
If your skin's clear and peachy,
don't taunt us, be glad.
We are plagued with a nightmare
that you've never had.

PEACEFUL COMPANION

In the warmth of my slumber I glance
at your face shining bright in the sky.
As I stare I drift into a trance
while the grey swirling clouds pass you by.

You look undisturbed and so tranquil
in the starry black velvet of night.
You sit in the heavens, majestic,
ne'er presenting a more graceful sight.

Through my window your moonlight engulfs me.
From the room we slip quietly away
to a land of deep thoughts and opinions
that can never be found in the day.

You make me relax, far from anguish,
a peaceful companion up high.
Soon my eyelids are heavy – I feel drowsy.
Back in my warm slumber I lie.

THIS EMPTY MAN

Would that I could change my life
to make my dreams come true.
I would sacrifice all wealth and fame
to hold, for always, you.

My sorrow lingers day and night,
to assail when thoughts set free.
My soul tormented weeps in vain
for what can never be.

If I could, by sorcery, start afresh
and mould this life my way,
you're the only fortune I would seek
and that none would take away.

The only sin of which I'm guilty
was to see your lovely face.
Now I roam forever punished
in the cell of my disgrace.

So please forgive this lonely man
if he sits alone, depressed.
Forgive these lost and saddened eyes
her image once caressed.

RESPLENDENT WITHIN REPUTATION

The mariner's found a harbour,
his maiden voyage complete.
For a lifetime he has changed;
with his youth he is estranged –
a culmination leading
to a glorious retreat.

What was lost he never wanted
and he'll never have again.
One great mystery is solved
and the truth has now evolved.
The question mark has vanished
from where it lingered until then.

No longer plagued with hunger
for that he could not seize,
he can raise his head with pride;
with his fate he did confide.
The torment rife inside him
he could finally appease.

TWENTIETH-CENTURY LEGEND

From October 1940
soon the world would realise
from a humble acorn
a giant oak would rise –
a courtroom jester
with aggression running wild,
thoughts of deep emotion
guided like a child,
worshipped by the legions
as to the top you rose.
A quartet revolution –
long hair and pointed toes.
Surrounded by immortals,
with flowers at your feet,
the psychedelic image
without you was incomplete.
Stood upon the Apple
with disciples down below,
it was time to end the chapter,
it was time for you to grow.
The pacifist campaigner –
words of wisdom in the air.
The world that was imagined
was way beyond compare.
At last they gave approval –
the dream had now come true –
with green card and a family,
the chance to start anew.
But as you tried to make a comeback,
four decades had gone by.
By the assassin you were greeted
and the world was left to cry.

CAT-AND-MOUSE GAME
(A poem for a male chauvinist)

Why can't you believe in lust at first sight?
Is the question that runs through my mind.
All that wining and dining just for one night.
The whole thing frustrating, I find.

It takes near a lifetime to get anywhere –
you've got to be subtle and sly.
To get any further's a question of dare,
but choose the right moment to try.

It's a pain in the neck all this playing hard to get.
Why can't she just stop all the pretence?
You've had one thing in mind since the first time you met.
Bit by bit you break down her defence.

The whole thing's a ludicrous cat-and-mouse game –
she knows what you're after; you're thinking the same.
It's almost a ritual to tempt and to tease,
and once that's all over you do as you please.

Sometimes you conclude you've just wasted your time –
a relationship pointless from start.
If it was worth all the waiting for, that would be fine.
Now it's time to move on – you depart.

THE SOLDIER'S LAMENT

To those who die
and those who cry
I drink this mournful toast.
The grief I feel
is oh too real;
it haunts me like a ghost.

This dreadful waste –
a frightening taste
of conflict's grim expense
as does this gloom
young souls consume
to leave a pain immense.

With deep regret
their fate is met,
life's secret now disclosed.
I curse in vain
a world insane,
its men in death reposed.

THE GAMBLER

You tried to win the people,
take their minds off growing strife.
To keep your head you gambled
with the stakes of human life.
In an act of desperation,
your cherished power on the wane,
like a gambler's greed for winning,
your ace card, this mad campaign,
already in the gutter
as the economy decayed.
Your country you had placed there;
on its patriots now you preyed.
This political manoeuvre,
as a means to save your face,
just created pointless bloodshed
and your country in disgrace.
While the nations mourn their losses,
on your shoulders rests the blame.
All those men now only memories;
to gain support your selfish aim.
With such bloody confrontation,
does your achievement make you proud –
to have caused so much bereavement,
to have formed this hateful cloud?

STYAL TRIAL

Deep in the night,
under moon shining bright
and the safe sheltered world left behind,
there is fear all around,
in every movement, every sound,
as the dark plays its tricks on the mind.

At the yard in the chill,
near the church all is still,
with low mist in the field by the well.
In the depth of the wood,
such a tense, wary mood,
on the path at the bridge in the dell.

THOUGHTLESS FEW

Those rowdy newts
and gaggling geese
invade the calm,
disturb the peace.
I ponder then
if roles turned round –
if they would curse
that raucous sound.

Such careless fools
with voices loud
encroach my quiet,
sleepy shroud.
Artistic tongues
care not for those
who in their warm beds
try to doze.

DRINKING MAN'S PLIGHT

At times I wonder why I drink,
as I kneel on the floor with my face in the sink.
A self-induced illness leaves me grumpy and frail.
I look like a zombie, unstable and pale.

I wave farewell to brain cells lost;
for a good night out, this dismal cost,
with a head pulsating, mouth all sour
and waves of nausea every hour.

Conversation a struggle, I sit head in hand.
My brain near explodes if I venture to stand.
Though hunger is nagging, the thought makes me ill,
of bacon and sausage, or cheese in the grill.

Whenever hung-over or sick on the night,
I swear to abandon this drinking man's plight.
Yet no sooner forgotten I'm out once again
to repeat that condition so dreaded till then.

TOMORROW

All this time I'm waiting,
my direction still unclear,
with no foreseeable future
and no known course to steer.

I am lost within my lifetime;
there is nowhere I can turn.
When asked of my intentions,
for an answer sound I yearn.

A career is what I search for,
but tomorrow looks to be
a frameless, empty picture.
There seems little there for me.

TRAIN TO FREEDOM

Are you listening to me carefully?
Are you trying to see the sights?
There's a thousand places burning
with a thousand neon lights.
Are you looking for adventure?
Are the pavements made of gold?
It's a land of dreary backstreets,
where lives are bought and sold.
Standing with your suitcase and your ticket,
at last you've finally come to find your dreams.
But don't you know before your travel's over
you'll find nothing here is ever as it seems?
You walk around so lonely
in the middle of the night.
You search for your new future,
but nothing comes in sight.
Do your parents wonder with tearful eyes
what it was they did so wrong?
If only you could realise
it's with them that you belong.
Sleeping in a doorway or bedsitter,
slaving part-time jobs to keep you fed,
wondering where the glitter disappeared to,
thoughts of leaving going through your head.
So go back to the station
with your suitcase in your hand.
Home is what you long for –
only now you understand.
Just board the train to freedom
and leave your dreams behind.
Then ask yourself the question,
how you could have been so blind.

SOON

Soon the night will turn to day.
Soon the black will pale to grey.
Soon the fear will be chased away.
Soon the lost will find their way.

Soon the sleeping will awake.
Soon the smiles as the new dawns break.
Soon the chills will the warm sun take.
Soon our lives will a fresh start make.

Soon the enemy will become a friend.
Soon on love will this world depend.
Soon will our fate lie around the bend.
Soon we'll hold hands and wait for the end.

INSPIRATION FROM THE PAST

Should I find myself deserted,
should I ever stand alone
on the street of hate and solitude
with its lost forbidding tone.

Should depression plague my daytime,
should my worries haunt my sleep,
I would live once more the memories
that my heart shall always keep.

You alone could lift my burdens.
You alone could ease the strain.
Just to see once more your image
warms my soul and soothes the pain.

You're my candle in the darkness
and my shelter in the storm.
Deep within my bleakest moment
I find comfort in your form.

Should I ever be downhearted,
should I ever give up hope,
as long as I remember you
for always I will cope.

Should the future bring me hardship,
should I feel too weak to last,
once more my heart will find
my inspiration from the past.

DIVINE EXEMPTION

Never try to tell me
that the way of life is just.
There is no reward for goodness;
there is no more room for trust.
Despite a person's kindness,
their desire to help and please,
there is no divine exemption
from hardship or disease.
If there was a Holy Father,
how could He sit up high,
allowing such unfairness –
to see good people cry?

THE UNION CARD

Some people claim the unions have a power much too strong,
a constant source of trouble to the state.
These people look with anger at the pickets in the cold –
a challenge to their 'freedom', which they hate.

Do the same staunch anti-unionists, working through a strike
while others forfeit money in their cause,
refuse the pay rise offered, for which colleagues had to fight,
or reap their share with shameless greedy claws?

Of course the union system has its problems, has its faults.
Perfection is so very hard to find.
But consider how things might be if employers had no threat.
To workers' needs no doubt they would be blind.

You need only look to history, before the unions formed,
to see conditions working classes faced.
Then maybe all those people who curse the union card
may condemn no more their power with such haste.

WINTER-MORNING BLUES

Oh Lord, how I hate
to get up in the morning,
the red sky displaying
its wintry warning.
My breath, like a mist,
through the chill floats away.
Beneath my warm covers
I wish I could stay.
With goosebumps and shivers,
half sleeping I clothe –
a ritual so often performed,
which I loathe.

THE CAT AND THE LION

So much of myself my eyes see in you.
I find it uncanny – too close to be true.
It is almost unnerving comparing each trait:
the things we find pleasing, the things that we hate.

We revel in comfort; agitation we scorn.
Both prone to mishaps since the day we were born.
Alone though not lonely, with hardly a sound
we prefer to move light, observe all around.

The signals of trouble we see at a glance;
with caution prevailing, leave nothing to chance.
Inquisitive ramblers, through instinct explore
whatever is hidden; we seek to know more.

The cat and the lion, though far from the same,
both share silent wishes, between us one aim.
To move with the current; our green eyes to see,
a future contented, for you and for me.

THE DEATH OF A POET

How can I think with a head full of thoughts?
The sum of my efforts, a puzzle of noughts.
From lost inspiration the question remains:
could this be the death of a poet?

Paper is empty, my pen lies unused –
victims of latent expression bemused.
Orphans, abandoned and gathering dust,
awaiting the death of a poet.

A FAITH BETRAYED

Please let me be dreaming
and soon to awake.
This feeling inside me
I gladly forsake.
The cruellest of nightmares,
it pains to believe.
For once how I hope
that these eyes do deceive.

Much more than the truth
does a faith betrayed hurt.
When lies are discovered
they stifle like dirt.
My heart becomes heavy
when no longer blind
to deceitfulness by those
I treated so kind.

The scar left within me
is ugly and deep –
to have my emotions
valued so cheap.
The users, abusers
I meet to regret;
I can do nothing more
than try and forget.

TRUE ESCAPE

To wander far in fields of thought,
through boundless lands of dreams.
So much to do, but never fraught,
where all is as it seems.

To hide away, for true escape
from all you cannot bear;
deep in the valleys of your mind,
no further look than there.

THE FOULEST OF FOUR-LETTER WORDS

Whoever first said that to live you must work
stands out as history's number-one berk.
He should have been taken and dropped in a pit,
mocked and insulted then covered in MUCK!
Overtime, flexitime, straight nine to five,
gnaws at the pleasure of being alive.
Who needs the hassle and earache from others?
The air of frustration entangles and smothers.
Tension that makes the adrenalin run free.
The Butterfly Boogie – who needs it? Not me.
I wake in the morning all comfy and snug,
like the proverbial bug in a rug.
The world of my making I leave in my bed
and head for another less friendly instead.
'Look on the bright side.' To cheer up I strive.
'I can call it a day when beyond sixty-five.'
After wasting a third of my life I retire.
I can slip on my slippers and snooze by the fire.
Christ, what a way to exist in my prime –
a slave to employment, that hideous crime!
If I won the pools in no office I'd rough it.
With a smile and two fingers I'd tell them to stuff it.
Early retirement would come in a flash;
like an Olympian athlete, I'd leave with a dash.
For now, sad to say, things will stay as they are.
I doubt my ambitions will get very far.
I am but a spot on Humanity's bum –
to remain Mr Nobody, under the thumb.
Ah well, at the weekend at least I can rest,
till that worm-ridden Monday gets me depressed.
Assembled, the multitude travel in herds.
'Work' is the foulest of four-letter words.

UNSUSPECTING ANGELS

A stagnant soul lies prostrate,
like a corpse upon the floor,
as scum around misuses
and diseases every pore.
Parasitic creatures slither;
Unsuspecting angels smile.
Soon their blood the leeches sample;
see them grinning, false and vile.
From the gutter they come crawling,
to plague the trusting breed.
Like vultures they devour them
in displays of mindless greed.
Those who know not how to surface
from the quicksands of our race,
in the sickly stench, so helpless,
disappear to leave no trace.

STUNNING CHARM

No artist could on canvas paint,
through words no writer say,
how beauty knows of no restraint;
it does on you array.

You smile and move with stunning charm,
in radiance always shown.
The strongest heart you soon disarm.
With warmth your presence known.

HELPLESS SITUATION

How soon you know the ending,
though the trip has just begun,
with so many things depending
on illusions in the sun.
There is nothing but uncertainty
spreading all around –
a piercing cold awareness
with no sanctuary found.
Such a helpless situation –
you are doomed to lose the fight,
but you keep determination,
holding on with all your might.
Your lifeline is diminished
as on and on you tread.
Your journey one day finished.
There is little hope ahead.

PEER'S PEST

Oh, yapping dog,
do please be still!
Awake I lie,
though not through will.
Incessant barking
spoils my rest.
'Tis thanks to you,
my canine pest.

This blissful lull
so oft you break.
Do pray desist
for goodness' sake.
How can I drift
to welcomed sleep
when to my ears
your noise does creep?

WITHOUT YOU

I miss you every lonely
empty second I must spend.
These hours are cold and dark
without my lover and my friend.

Each day is like a lifetime
filled with sadness and despair.
This week will seem eternal –
no longer could I bear.

When you return my sky will clear,
eclipsed no more by sorrow.
Then once again I'll smile and face
a brighter warm tomorrow.